Dark Miracle

Dark Miracle

A collection of new poems by Jung Hyunwoo
Translated by Sunnie Chae

검은 기적 정현우

K-Poet Series 047
ASIA

Contents

Cucumber Soap	8
Planarian	10
Pomegranate	12
Gaji	14
Mourning	16
Things that Don't Change after Death	18
Pillow	20
Winter Prayer	22
Roseville—for H	26
Inheritance	28
Rose Forest	30
Roseville	32
Roseville	34

Litmus	36
Tarot Cards and All Dice	38
Roseville	42
Roseville	46
Curtain of Butterflies and Moths—Roseville	48
Plant Parent	50
In Her Arms	54
Poet's Note	57
Poet's Essay	61
Commentary	83

DARK MIRACLE

POET

Cucumber Soap

This cucumber soap belonged to Mom

When I wash my face
The green hue still remains
The soft foam of an un-soft world still remains
I wonder about sorrow
Faithfully surviving a pale form that dissolves

One blinding summer day in the cucumber patch
She hid among vines to peel and pickle
Her small hand passing me pieces

Cucumbers piled perilously high

Summer rain blurred the window
Shades of elusive green slipped by
Sunlit vines glimmered white and climbed

Wake up, open your eyes
O, I shook Mom's shoulders
That day, she would no longer rise
That day, her breath withered inward
Green flesh filled with bruised light

O, feeble beauty
The cucumber soap drops to my feet
I fall to my knees and weep

Planarian

Light leaves behind a watery trail.
A life-form embracing its undoing,
it grows an arm, generates a leg.

On Easter, my sister speaks of the dead.
Do fingers fall from prayer I've forsaken?

Church organs of memory lose fingers too.
Shattered eggshells never fully reattach.

Black organ keys vanish,
walls push away traces of night.
Between heart and severed soul
sprout sutures of clear thread.

Shades of summer sing low.

Pomegranate

Carols ring out for the holidays,
red cherry lights flicker in the square.
I part ways with my lover and buy
twelve pomegranates whole.

I kneel, facing a world torn open
by hands you pulled along.

Lists of sins pierce through me,
embers batter my body.
Stunned by sorrow and searing sun,
my blood-crusted heart cries mercy,
rolls to your feet.

And you, seeking salvation,
swallow all the broken fruit.

Gaji*

You, gaji, stroking an eggplant's violet skin,
your heart collapsing, you go,
on an evening of swollen love and fruit,
like eggplants sold by the roadside.
You mutter it wasn't meant to be,
the saddest taste in your mouth, you go,
each moment recounted, root to fruit,
with teeth, clear bones, gnawing at my edges.
Plum-colored shell, toughened in shade,
caressing bruises on flesh, you go.
Mom stir-fried eggplant when she lived,

  * *Gaji* can mean *eggplant, to go*, or *branch*; the word also appears in idiomatic expressions that extend or modify the sense of *go*.

gaji, her soft voice on your tongue, you go,
you, gaji, recalling an eggplant dinner, you go,
The sunset purples with puckery sorrow,
vines from Mom's body branch skyward.
Gaji, seeking naked silence,
you, gaji, bridging and balancing worlds.

Between my eyes bloodshot,
somewhere down the middle,
a hairline crack, gaji will go.

Mourning

I dismembered a doll,
one limb at a time.

I removed the eyelids,
plucked the dreams inside.

Dreams shriveled like seeds,
I watered the hollows.

Hushed, I rejoined the neck,
refitted hands and feet,
but memory unglued.

My hands, pricked,

refused to bleed.

I left the tail end of thread
to linger on like sorrow,
wound day after day
around my finger.

On and off,
it beat with my pulse.

Things that Don't Change after Death

Sorrow sits at the table, day and night,
never setting down its spoon.

My face mirrors on a red surface,
tears thinning into strands
like noodles unraveled by chopsticks.

I survive, stirring soup into my rice
as if sinning by living.

Mom's funeral was followed by rain.

The old dog runs through puddles
only to circle back—but why.

The birds perched on power lines
are all said to cry—but why.
The lids over our eyes
are meant to shut—but why.

I count on my fingers the things
that don't change after death.

Hunger finds me again tonight.

Pillow

Strangely, though Mom died,
I slept well.
I wept in dreams, my pillow dry.

The pillow granted peace,
and by being alive,
I felt warm,
and for that, sorrier.

Winter Prayer

When Mom had only a week to live,
I stood in the dark dead center of winter.
I stood as if not knowing how to weep.

Winter passes in summer's shadow.
Lord, if there is breath to spare,
will you let me hear Mom's heart?
My sister is set against life support.
Lord, God withholding Your image,
am I undeserving of a miracle?
How do I acquiesce without going mad
while Mom still breathes?
When unclosing eyes fall shut,
the window glares into sorrow's new eyes

that I draw and offer in prayer.

When snow blankets a body overnight,
do not promise wonders,
do not demand my faith.
Chairs left empty as if sitters rose when called,
traces of bygone doors and bells,
streets of untrodden snow,
carols of a solitary night,
carols of a night.
Someone steps out the door—

Ah, Mom died this summer.

Alone, I eat a bowl of rice.

Tap, tap,

spilling like grain,

snow falls at the window.

Roseville—for H

Rain ripped into streaks to hang from the roof.
A silent heart caved in the afternoon.
I muttered the names of things that fell.
Names soaked in fire, recalled in rain.
The blue gate, grown over with moss,
the windows unlit, tearstained.
It rained that day too.
Flood water rose in the town,
a boy's marbles buried in the ground
stayed safe as the dark overflowed.
Splashes slipped into eyelids,
pooling deeper than memory.
Names reversed or sank in water,
the town's name nearly washed away.

The boy held a marble up to the sun.
Rain wept even in that sphere.
The glow belonged to no one,
impure, nebulous feeling.
The heart designed to always rain
made veiny paths in the glass,
charting a yet-unspeaking soul.
Gazing into the grayish marble,
that embryonic heart,
the boy believed in his being.
Something survived unshattered,
and from that, an indelible story.

Inheritance

Mom,
I had never written your name so many times.
Headed home after canceling your phone, I'm
   on my way,
buying heart-shaped persimmons on my way,
passing streetlamps glowing overripe on my way.
Holding your phone in shadows,
I know,
the voice I hear is my own.

A long, quiet road leads to persimmons.
Look, seeds—I carry on as if in penance.
O, round time—
Mom, your evening closed with persimmon

flowers.

Forgive me—I can only pen so much with my
  sorrow,
though I recall the summer hues when you
  lived.

You died when persimmons were ripe.
In my dreams, you will have a basket full,
red-orange fruit spilling, spilling out—

Rose Forest

Every day after she died, I took out her heart
and held it up to the window light.

The heart fractured once a day,
shards more honest than confession.
In light, the heart appeared almost human.

In rose season, it crimsoned.

When the heart no longer bled,
I placed it in a glass box.
It glimmered and seemed to harden.
Then something began to sprout.

Finger-like tendril, slender and soaked in tears, trembled more like eyelids than leaves, curling shut when brushed by light. Dried in the sun, the heart grew clear and filled with frail thorns. I passed through that forest, stroking its shadows until softly cast out. In the heart stood a red door, and beyond it, a quieter forest. Behind eyes shut by sorrow, it took shape.

Roseville

Christmas Day, only one house had a candle in the window. Three o'clock in the afternoon, the church bells rang. I walked south past the sewing factory, toward the fossil graves. Snow had fallen since dawn. From the northern hill, I saw what I used to see, icicles brought down a roof, but no one stirred in the village. Christmas evening, I recalled Mother's cross-stitch pattern. A small holly tree, a baby in a manger, a scene with no one in tears. That year, Mother had sat like a sewing box, winding balls of thread. I watched as faces once lost were slowly woven in. The thread never unraveled and never reached an end. It stretched out as night fell slower than snow. By dark, the snow reached my knees. With the candle lit, I saw things Mother had not managed to mend, things too soaked for her needle yet bound by colored thread. In every house, doors sealed shut with hushed shadows. The needle's eye was too small, but I could not hear her call for me. I did not turn back.

Roseville

When they pulled her drowned body from the
    shallows,
they said the nameless woman wore a face
so peaceful, so serene.

From the garden of a deserted house
drifted the scent of unripe peaches.
Bruised and green, with something astir
beneath the flesh.
Tiny cocoon of a peach moth.
I unpicked the stitches of its pillowcase.

Stationary in still life,
things would still speak.

Litmus

Science lab—pale shadows melt into a glass beaker, bloodless yet looking like blood, until the transparent liquid is labeled tears. They say litmus paper comes from lichen, rootless carriers of long memory in low places, leaflessly breathing in colonies. Is joy the start, sorrow the end, with nothing hidden in between? Silent beneath a red traffic light, blue rainwater pools, clouds cluster and climb high. When I imagine the palm of the first litmus-testing alchemist, summer is buoyed between silence and glass, a candy of shards, a candle in a beaker. An unbeating heart warps the color that lived in eyes. When I hold a magnifying glass to burn feeler-like fingers choosing color, or the loosened hollow of secrets, I find a nameless blue insect that cannot fly. The waterdrop on paper needs no explaining, it has already begun. Living color, determined elsewhere. Why does red, eager to endure, turn sickly blue? Colorless light filters into the lab, like a caged bird asleep. Eyes shut, I find scenes I thought were lost, where colors hush and light fades. From there, again. Distilled light, salvation.

Tarot Cards and All Dice

1. Heatwave—one by one, sunflower seeds scatter into the pasture. Time transcribes false mortal sentences; numbers tell more honest lies. Zero—God has already turned, discerning deceit.

2. If God-given numbers prophesy, they do so as inscrutable inscriptions. Gravestones—numbers etched in single stroke, ending before things begin. The burial ground, still warm, obscures the living. Divinity dwells even among low numbers—yet invent them not.

3. Luck—stones cast at random, as with existence without reason, as with nightly questions in dreams, repetition lives only in numbers on dice. Trinity—an ancient fallacy describing deity.

4. Acrid odor of urine from my dead dog and Grandma—which is sadder, the one-eyed fish or her stare? Every puncture of sorrow leads to another. Follow the tears down, through bygone days unborn. Dreams cushion the landing.

5. A bird blinks its left eye, then its right, and

the horizon misaligns. Five fingers—none of
them take after the divine.

6. Cube—center collapsing before the will, no
two-footed support for the world. Balance
tilts to the side. Memory—a mistake in
probability.

7. I want a number not among these.

Roseville

A cotton tree forest I had never seen
unfurls its doors for me.
The forest ripples
like entrails in the body.
It swallows the snowstorm
never stopping for breath.
The snow has yet to fall
but it learns to disremember.
Severed ears sprout on branches,
ruptured eardrums open like wounds
where salamanders crawl.
A tree drips glassy gel from its eyes
onto a hand half-buried.
I cannot inter or interrogate,

and yet,

I grasp it and gaze.

Like silken threads sparking feeble light,

it bears frail warmth of the departed.

Along crusted arteries,

flame-like tails slice through tree veins.

The forest, half-dead

and I, in between

nearly broken

nearly awoken

a sound unreached by tongue

a song throatless in time

a name uncalled—

Perhaps

this forest is somebody's dream.

Roseville

Beneath the window, I found a fallen fruit.
The pod was half open, its seeds flushed red
like faces holding breath
underwater.

Once the silk tree slept,
arrowroot vines crept up the window,
drawing the darkness inside.

A door creaked open down the hall.
Plants forgot by sealing shut,
memory held out longer.

Leaves sprouted from hands of the dead. Over

time, plants furled inward, no one spoke of
death, yet all things were remembered. In
the windowless hall, an abandoned box held
a doll with six fingers and black seeds in her
pocket. Roseville's ground floor, first to catch
the sun, last to stay dark.

Burnt roof, ashen under snow. People I saw
yesterday brushed past me today. Down
the hall at night, there used to be a star
chart. Residents left unwatered plants out
their doors. They neither thrived nor died.
Something inside somehow survived.

Curtain of Butterflies and Moths—Roseville

Room steeped in the scent of old candles, a rose painting hanging from the wall. Glimpse of a mailbox, likely empty of letters. The window opens, we rise in hushed flight through vapor trails. No wings, no hands, bodies shrinking, we out-soar shadows past hills, houses, stagnant hours. Never arriving, never turning back. Grazing broken glass on walls, unharmed. Winter coats wait on a clothesline. We exist outside light. All in quiet order.

Behind the curtain, scaly-winged lepidopterans inch together. I fail to tell apart butterflies and moths, the living and left behind. Outside the window, lifeless trees sway. Wallpaper peels in a corner. Birds without legs fold themselves by. When held by the tip, their wings measure distance and light. Strands of sunlight silently unravel. Interred bodies bear a loved one's face. Eyes shut, we speak for long.

Plant Parent

Seaweed in soup is no plant.
It's simple enough to say
as sunlit possibility moves overhead.
Wide window of refracted light fills my view,
but the refraction is no being.
Outside of speed and time,
I dwell on what is no plant, animal, or spore,
    but seaweed and slipper animalcule, algal
    and protozoan masses, mind multiplying ad
    infinitum as I empty my bowl of seaweed
    soup.
I place a cup of water next to the humidifier.
Yesterday, I saw tear stains,
perhaps with stems inside.

Today, I look longer,
only to hear the doctor say
the body will no longer stave off sleep.
Survival, a fractional possibility.
If the death-claimed is no plant or person,
sunbeams unspool, showering or crisscrossing
    rain, a hand waves down the corridor, no life
    line creased, days pass in the ward with no
    word of light, only a slumberous, vegetative
    mouth, thoughts easily torn and outstripped
    by grief—these are my lies.

I draw the curtain to let in the light.
Past the hygrometer, around Mom's mouth,

I hold my palm.

In Her Arms

My dog died three years past.

Now Mom has passed too,
and she will embrace
my little dog.

Closed in her coffin,
but in an open dream,
I place the pup in her arms
and return.

POET'S NOTE

I raced until her breath gave out.

The road to the hospital loomed, an endless dawn, and fearing

her heart would stop if I arrived, I raced wishing I never would.

All lights failed as I pressed my ear to her chest and caught

the last tremor. It taught me

the lie

that love beats death.

I had finally arrived,

and her breathing ceased.

In her eyes, I saw myself forlorn.

Eyes that had waited for mine,

eyes that discerned certain death.

Son, let me leave.

I will turn the road of no return,

relive through your eyes,
reunite with you in distant time.

When I close my eyes,
I see her reborn.

This collection of poems I dedicate to her,
the greatest, most sacred and beloved being in my life.

POET'S ESSAY

Notes of a Dark Miracle

May 28, 2024

They say she will die.

The words are far too simple.

An unbearable darkness unfolds.

May 29, 2024

I watched her wrestle with death.

I could only pray to a God I did not believe.

May 30, 2024

"Her brain is gone."

Not even a one-percent chance.

Memory, a useless, abandoned house.

Beyond comprehension, beyond reach.

May 31, 2024

They said she wouldn't last three days, but today is the fourth.

She sleeps as peacefully as a child.

As I dozed beside her, I thought I heard murmurs behind me.

Everything was rewritten and rearranged.

June 1, 2024

I think of sentences trembling with ambivalence and melancholy.

The language quivers like nerves,

thrashing at the cliff's edge of pathological mourning.

The path I seek lies elsewhere.

I wish for sentences that lead mourning to completion,

language that seizes yet surpasses sorrow, reaching beyond transience toward transcendence.

June 2, 2024
She seems a plant.
I shake her shoulders, yet she will not wake.
My heart caves in, but breath continues.

June 3, 2024
How much of myself had leaned on her?
Can I persist as myself in her absence?
There will be no one-percent miracle.
She has taught me joy.
In the end, she teaches me sorrow.

June 4, 2024
In *aedo*, or "mourning," the *ae* (哀) of "sorrow"

seems less fitting than the *ae* (愛) of "love."

Her love for me was vast; the heart I return is pitifully small.

June 6, 2024 (Dawn)

Many came to visit in the hospital.

I know she will not wake, yet I sign a CPR consent form.

Against the odds, I place all my hope on fingertips.

June 9, 2024 (Morning)

I think of joy and calamity.

Her looming death is a calamity that reshapes all of time.

Mere survival can be a joy. It can.

June 9, 2024 (Day)

Today, as I make notes on methods of mourning,

I realize they are more than cold, theoretical sentences.

Freud's voice echoes, distinguishing mourning from melancholia.

From him, I learn about loss as a trace etched in the heart,

not the mere absence of an object.

In Lacanian terms, the loss of libido,

words searing like undying embers.

Somewhere, love's flame still burns.

June 9, 2024 (Night)

I fell asleep beside her.

Hands held, we walked into a snowy forest.

She quickened her steps and outpaced me.

I called her name, but she never looked back.

June 10, 2024

I put on her favorite song, "All I Want for Christmas Is You."

The singer and I share the same prayer.

June 11, 2024

I watched the moment her breath ceased.

The God I had loved, I now blamed.

I stood, wretched, before immense grief.

June 12, 2024 (Dawn)

I returned to the house where we had lived.

I changed the door lock's PIN.

Overnight, I told her the new code in my dream.

Without a word, she smiled.

June 12, 2024 (Day)

Sorting her belongings, I came across her tidy handwriting.

My name appeared here and there in her notebook.

Then, blank pages that were never turned.

June 13, 2024

I wonder: do human sentiments dwell in the heart or the brain?

I fleetingly feel unafraid of death.

One question remains: what does it mean to be human?

June 14, 2024

The house is too quiet. I cover my ears in silence.

There is sorrow in the fact that my anxiety will

persist.

June 14, 2024

Mourning is an emotional calamity that arrives in abrupt parting.

Novels examine the consumption and erasure of public mourning;

poetry confronts the consumption of emotions tied to personal loss.

The novel is social and political; poetry, intensely personal.

June 15, 2024

I cooked rice. Out of habit, I set her spoon on the table.

I took Mom's side dishes from the refrigerator, then returned them untouched.

June 17, 2024

My face in the mirror overlaps with hers.

I recall the doctor asking consent for organ donation.

If only I had transplanted a part of her into my body.

How strange to think her entire being is gone.

June 18, 2024

I walked past a local flower shop with rows of white chrysanthemums.

The world flows on, as if eternal.

June 19, 2024

She held me close in a dream.

Her arms were so cold that I woke and wept.

June 20, 2024

Auntie called. "Are you all right?" she asked.
Of course not. But I replied, "Yes."

June 22, 2024

In her room, I noticed the hat she often wore.
The scent of her hair, of summer.

June 24, 2024

On the street, I saw a man walking hand in hand with his aging mother.

A scene denied to me.

June 25, 2024

Poetry seems less an emotional outpouring than an emotional arrangement.

The more scattered the feelings, the calmer the language.

Since her passing, I am relearning how to

speak.

June 26, 2024

To accept death as another sentiment perhaps means discovering a feeling still alive.

My language halts where she has vanished.

I cannot speak, yet the silence somehow fills me.

June 27, 2024

The world drowns my sorrow.

Fumbling after it, I glimpse the ruins of shadows.

I reach for the shards, but they cut my hand.

June 28, 2024

It rained through the night. I trace rain streaks on the window, but they vanish.

My face appears, then disappears. The world beyond the glass vanishes,

questions and emptiness remain.

June 30, 2024

I moved the side dishes Mom had made from the refrigerator to the freezer.

I read the dates written on each lid.

How long is their shelf life?

The shelf life for Mom and me has reached an end.

July 2, 2024

I read a book of poems. To read and write poetry feels like a luxury.

July 3, 2024

I took her scarf from the closet and wrapped it

around my neck.

Mom's winter scent lingered.

Her hands were always so cold.

I probably never told her I loved her.

Instead, I held her hand.

July 5, 2024

I passed by the hospital.

My body trembled at the sound of an ambulance.

I am still trapped in that day.

July 6, 2024

I cannot look straight at her photos.

Time without her, devoid of joy and sorrow,

is time when I am wholly myself.

July 7, 2024

Today, I read Derrida. To him, mourning precludes success or failure.

Melancholy lingers, a longing that stays.

I hold onto those words.

The dead never leave entirely.

Sometimes in dreams, sometimes in sentences, they speak.

July 8, 2024

It occurred to me today.

The dead do not go far.

They stay between sentences,

living quietly with our breath.

July 9, 2024

The village dog barked. I cried too, I think, but could not hear myself weep.

July 10, 2024

I try to pen poems, but sentences refuse.

This seems part of the poems.

Language disappears when words fail,

but a deep breath-like something takes its place.

Perhaps poetry records that breath.

July 12, 2024

I opened Mom's notebook on my desk. She had written my name as if calling a child.

July 15, 2024

Mom had boiled three eggs, her last batch.

Sam, the number three, *samsin*, the Trinity, and Samsun, Mom's name.

July 17, 2024

Before canceling Mom's phone, I left her a voice message.

"I'm sorry you had to work too hard all your life. Sleep well."

August 3, 2024
I unlocked Mom's cell phone. I saw old texts she had sent to me.

August 5, 2024
A cicada cried from the tree outside the house.
The cry called forth summers of my childhood.

August 7, 2024
I saw so many stars in the night sky.
They seemed like Mom's eyes.
I counted them as I fell asleep.

August 9, 2024

I sat in the living room with the lights turned off.

It felt as if Mom were asleep in the bedroom, so I held my breath.

August 10, 2024

Mom smiled in my dream.

When I see her face,

my heart aches, as I know it's a dream.

August 12, 2024

Today I revisited mourning.

The shock of loss prompts inexplicable sorrow

to seep through the body like water through cotton.

It weighs my mind and body down.

August 14, 2024

To write a poem of mourning is to offer
a poetic reply to the question: how shall one heal?
The answer is not born of reason,
but of diary-like notes and confessions.

August 18, 2024

I live leaning on things being forgotten.
But the sorrow of her loss will endure, no matter the time.

August 20, 2024

Melanie Klein traced mourning back to a child's cry.
The infant's tears shed in the mother's absence,
that primal sorrow already holds the origin of mourning.

Levinas spoke of the gaze that beholds
another's death.
If I could shatter myself,
I would gather the torn fragments
and make my way toward wholeness.

August 24, 2024
To mourn is not to grieve
but to hold another heart that keeps breathing.
There is hope that, in loss, another name
might be born.

August 30, 2024
When I think of her, I'm overcome by longing
and resentment, love and rage.
As if bundled into a single nerve, those
emotions tremble through me.
At times, the trembling feels like an illness.

In seizing and surpassing sorrow, perhaps I prove I am alive.

September 20, 2025
Strangely, though Mom died, I slept well.
That night, when everything collapsed,
I lay my head against the pillow and fell asleep.
My body, the blanket, the air—all warm.
It sank me deeper into slumber.
As I closed my eyes, it felt like Mom's warmth and made me sorrier. Sorry that I was alive, falling so fast asleep.
That, I could not forgive.

October 10, 2025
When I close my eyes after crying, only my survival remains.
As I breathe, she dies and is reborn.

I will stop remembering her in writing.

And yet, I will inevitably write again.

The work of mourning and sustaining her falls on me.

COMMENTARY

Long Memory in Low Places

Kim Yeondeok (Poet)

Hyunwoo sunbae. The only person who calls me hoobae. And among all my seniors, the only one I call sunbae. The word evokes flowing fabric and a steadfast shadow. Perhaps that is why, even when you greeted everyone with gentle eyes and a smile, I imagined all the things passing through you. "Stationary in still life, / things would still speak," and so would your sorrow, quietly burning and turning transparent behind a veil ("Roseville"). In this new collection of poems, you speak calmly of still-life objects that resemble that sorrow: of fruits, colors, people, and small-bodied dreams. These stories scatter and gather under different light, always pointing to one person. Yes, the one you love most: your mother.

We live in a world too strange, too cruel—the "soft foam of an un-soft world" ("Cucumber Soap"). Waiting for us in that "un-soft world" are inexplicably fatal partings. After a long farewell to your mother, you grapple with guilt. You write, "Strangely, though Mom died, / I slept well"; "I survive, stirring soup into my rice / as if sinning by living" ("Pillow," "Things that Don't Change after Death"). You "carry on as if in penance," "kneel, facing a world torn open by hands [she] pulled along," confessing, "lists of sins pierce through me" ("Inheritance," "Pomegranate," ibid.). From these pangs of conscience, your poetry begins. There is self-reproach for sustaining one's life after a loved one's death, sensations that intrude and mingle with mourning, and the ache of being ajar with the world. You must have sat there, enduring it all.

I wonder how you chose "Cucumber Soap" as the opening poem. As an object that once belonged to your mother, the fragrant bar conjures memories of how she used to "peel and pickle" cucumbers; it also awakens the senses to your final moments together, when "green flesh filled with bruised light." It links you, the living, to your mother beyond time, a bridge at once wounding and healing. Reading this ode to "feeble beauty," I imagine you standing with eyes closed, unable to summon or touch the one you love, yet still bathed in a soft afterglow. That glowing light takes on many forms: colorful fruits, including cucumbers, pomegranates, eggplants, and persimmons, "Mother's cross-stitch pattern," "traces of bygone doors and bells" ("Roseville," "Winter Prayer"). From these emerges the "sorrow / faithfully surviving a pale form that dissolves" ("Cucumber Soap").

What are light and form to you, sunbae? Surely not ideas but living, moving scenes, bearing the vivid weight of reality made possible by your loved one. Now that you have parted, those scenes will never be the same. In the sequence "Roseville," titled after the place where she lived and where you spent time together, the speaker observes, "Roseville's ground floor, first to catch the sun, last to stay dark." Yet this sunlit space turns into one where "light leaves behind a watery trail," now the "dark dead center of winter" ("Planarian," "Winter Prayer").

Once light passes, the spirit and heart

helplessly left behind can only wait in that place. Not knowing how days slip by, seasons turn, and bodies change. You observe an unmoving heart in a glass box and wordlessly recall the warmth that once was. Then, within that still box, clear yet dark, and within your poems, the inexplicable unfolds. Though light and form are lost, the things inside that "somehow survived" come into being "outside of light" ("Roseville," "Curtain of Butterflies and Moths—Roseville"). This remarkably resilient recovery appears as "sutures of clear thread" ("Planarian"). In the speaker's mind, this thread that "never unravel[s] and never reach[es] an end" lingers "like sorrow" and "beat[s] with my pulse" ("Roseville," "Mourning," ibid.). The thread even recovers "faces once lost . . . slowly woven in" ("Roseville"). Extending this motif, vines "branch skyward . . . bridging and balancing worlds," and "behind eyes shut by sorrow . . . t[ake] shape" ("Gaji," "Rose Forest").

When "strands of sunlight silently unravel," the glow "belong[s] to no one," and from that emerges "an indelible story" ("Curtain of Butterflies and Moths—Roseville," "Roseville—for H," ibid.). Thus your poetry becomes a collection of poems. What "t[akes] shape" as a book of illuminating, deep sorrow reaches readers, and me, in a place where "colors hush and light fades" ("Rose Forest," "Litmus"). In the fact that "something survive[s] unshattered," I sense "distilled light, salvation" ("Roseville—for H," "Litmus"). Perhaps this collection is your record of all that has been distilled. Distillation changes the light. Distilled light returns something to the bereaved, suggesting the freedom and warmth of possibility. Love continues among beloved beings: "closed in her coffin, / but in an open dream, / I place the pup in her arms / and return" ("In Her Arms").

Hyunwoo sunbae, you must have endured a long, long summer. Now winter returns. This winter, I hope to walk with you through streets as serene as that "quieter forest" in the heart ("Rose Forest"). The winter streets will freeze and thaw, remaining darker than summer while revealing far more. I hope to share stories about all things that carry "long memory in low places" ("Litmus"). I will trust those stories with you, my sunbae who walks with the sorrow, smile, and steps of one who remembers for long. Do tell me, in time, the neighborhood where you would like to walk.

K-POET 47
Dark Miracle

Written by Jung Hyunwoo
Translated by Sunnie Chae
Published by ASIA Publishers
Address 445, Hoedong-gil, Paju-si, Gyeonggi-do, Korea
Email bookasia@hanmail.net
ISBN 979-11-5662-317-5 (set) | 979-11-5662-810-1 (04810)
First published in Korea by ASIA Publishers 2025

*This book is published with the support of the Literature Translation Institute of Korea (LTI Korea).